The Power of Hybridization: Sharing Field Experiences in Project Management

Waterfalls and Whirlpools in Real Life

1st Edition - December 2023

Project Management Institute. France

The History of the Manuscript and Its Conception

On February 6, 2014, Stéphane DEROUIN (head of the **"Lab Hybrid"**) presented for the first time "officially" the theme of the hybridization of project modes at the ENSAM School of Engineer in Cluny. His conference was entitled: "Project management towards a new hybrid approach: Waterfall vs. Agile-Scrum".

Since 2014, to bring the subject to the forefront, we have collectively and individually led numerous initiatives in our professional networks and experiments with pioneering clients.

Persevering in our approach, strengthened by the publication of the PMBOK® Guide Seventh Edition, in August 2021, with a totally renewed approach integrating value management and tailoring, we have decided to launch an initiative with experienced project management professionals in France and to create a group entitled **"Lab Hybrid"**.

With the support of the then President of PMI France, Ricardo NACIFF, we have brought together, starting in September 2021, a multi-faceted team of about 30 people from all sectors of activity, some more experienced in traditional methods, others more Agilist, with the objective of creating a "hybrid best practices guide".

Here is the product of our collective work.

Table of Contents

Dedication

- Poem from Antonio MACHADO

This manuscript is dedicated to all project managers who are daily trying their best to turn ideas into actions and make it happen in real life... Project is a way, project is the way, and that way is made by walking!

Wayfarer, only your footprints
are the path, and nothing more,
· wayfarer, there is no path,
you make the path as you walk.

-Antonio Machado

Dear Reader,

if you are passionate about Project Management and wish to contribute to our **"Lab Hybrid"** adventure, do not hesitate to connect with the team: https://pmi-france.org/Lab-Hybrid

Acknowledgments

We would like to thank all the members of the "**Lab Hybrid**" who participated, and Stéphane DEROUIN, its initiator, as well as the PMI France and its Past President Ricardo NACIFF.

A "special thanks" to:

Estelle REMONDEAU (I3-CRG, CNRS, ÉCOLE POLYTECHNIQUE, INSTITUT POLYTECHNIQUE DE PARIS, France) for her help and presentation of her research: *"Is Agile development transferable to complex physical products development projects in industrial context? A comparative case study".*

&

Jean-Luc FAVROT (Member of PMI France - VP Horizon Branch - who contributed to the drafting of the PMBOK® Guide Seventh Edition) for his remarks and final proofreading.

About the Author

The following people were members (text or concept contributors) of the "**Lab Hybrid**" project core team responsible for writing the document, including reviewing and arbitrating recommendations to improve its content.

Who	Information	Photo
Delphine FALCOZ	With over 15 years of international industrial experience, Delphine founded the company Supp-Projects in 2019. She is a consultant and trainer in project management, as well as an outsourced project manager. Delphine holds certifications from PMI® (PMP - 2011 and Agile Hybrid Project Pro - 2022) and Scrum.org (PSM and PSPO - 2022) and is the author of the book "60 minutes to master your project deadlines" published by Gereso.	
Fernando MARI	Co-founder of IKIDO, a company specialized in ERP integration, Fernando has over twenty years of experience in the IT sector, particularly in software editors and integrators (HRIS and ERP) as a project manager. With a background in computer engineering, PMP certified since 2017, and with an international perspective, he currently holds dual roles as company executive and Sage X3 ERP integration project manager.	
François BUREAU	Agile Coach - Agricultural engineer, specialist in approaches to complex and changing environments. Founder, creator, administrator, contributor, and coordinator of the "Agile Coaching University" and "A l'Ecole de la V.I.E." websites. Popularizer and speaker on agile practices at scale and its main frameworks. Member of PMI, certified as PMP, PMI-ACP, PMI-RMP, DASM, SAFe SPC, PSM, PSD, PSK, PRINCE2, AgilePM, ITIL. Member of the "Accompagnement solidaire" collective and rugby enthusiast.	
Gaël DAVID	An engineer with a passion for projects, Gaël has worked for 20 years on industrial projects of various sizes in France and internationally, also gaining experience in portfolio management, coordination of project managers, and mentoring. He transmits this passion by training engineering students, focusing his interventions on project management methodologies and human management as vectors of change in organizations. In 2018, he joined PMI to develop and promote the PM profession, and to enrich himself through exchanges with his peers.	

Guénolé SAUREL

A computer engineer, Guénolé has been working in project management and telecoms for 20 years. Certified PMP, he has managed projects and programs for major clients of Orange Business Services. He is also an internal trainer in Waterfall project methodology and currently supports the transition of operational businesses (outside of IT and development) within the company towards agility and hybridization.

Hélène TERRIER

Hélène contributes her know-how in business, IT and project management to facilitate transformation and organization. She relies on her experience in the retail, supply chain, and manufacturing sectors, in support of cross-functional teams and specific processes, both in France and abroad, within groups, ETIs, and SMEs, to provide skills honed by 20 years of professional experience. Committed to driving value, she takes a proactive approach to balancing performance and sustainability.

Isabelle ICORD

Engineer in microelectronics, Isabelle has managed development projects for major French and American companies, for US and Japanese automotive markets, as well as in Europe for consumer, industrial, military, and aerospace sectors. She works to promote and implement Critical Chain through her company, Pro CC. She is the author of the book "Critical Chain in Practice" and a comprehensive online video training program, Boost Project System, and gives courses and lectures. Additionally, she is SMPP (Project Portfolio Management System) certified consultant.

Marylène LAFON

With an MBA from the University of South Alabama, USA, Marylène has over 20 years of professional experience as a business entity manager and operational team leader in IT transformation and digital innovation. She is PMP certified since 2001 and served as PMO leader, then Business and Operations Manager for IBM Global Services contract with Michelin worldwide for 10 years. As a consultant and trainer in Management and Projects, and affiliated professor with Groupe ESC Clermont for over 12 years, Marylène founded blubeige in 2022, a consulting and management training company.

Mathieu STOLTZ

Currently EPCI Director, Mathieu, graduated as engineer, has 26 years of international experience in the energy sector on construction sites and engineering centers. In particular, he has held numerous project management positions for the past 17 years, covering all types of onshore and offshore facilities in the design, development, and implementation phase. He has contributed as a mentor to project leadership development programs and won three corporate innovation awards related to team dynamics and individual flourishing within projects.

Michael SANCHEZ Founder of MS Consulting, a company specializing in project management with a strong digital component, Michaël has worked for over 20 years for clients of all sizes, including international institutions and start-ups with only a few employees, in various domains such as industry, banking, military, and government. Michaël holds certifications from PMI, Scrum.org, and Axelos.

Noémie VILLARD Following an experience as a system engineer, Noémie progressed to project management in the medical device field at a large international group in 2017. Since 2021, she has joined Merck Science and Lab Solution as PMO. Noémie has an Engineering degree and M.Sc. in medical engineering from Phelma (Grenoble INP) and KTH (Sweden). She has been practicing synchronized swimming for over 20 years.

Pascal BERAMIS An engineer, Pascal has been working as a Change Manager and consultant trainer in Management and Projects since 2012 (as the founder and CEO of BPE). His motto is: Make change a key element of differentiation and sustainable performance.

Stéphane DEROUIN Head of Practice at SCALIAN S&T, specialist in portfolio management and hybridization, Stéphane leads consulting missions and presents training sessions in all sectors of activity. In 1995, he was one of the seven founders of PMI in France, former President of the PMI® French Chapter, member of the Supervisory Board, and the "Lab Hybrid" leader. Certified Agile Project Management – AgilePM® from APMG International, and since 2018, he is a teacher and tutor for the Agile MSc® International Project Management program at ESCP.

Stéphane ROUSSEAU An engineer, PMP certified, and specialized in organizational transformation, Stéphane has over 20 years of hands-on experience in project management in industrial environments. He recently implemented a hybrid project management methodology in an environment where the very nature of the activities required hybridization, at the intersection of software, electronic, mechanical engineering, as well as all the professions linked to the industrialization of new products (manufacturing, testing, methods, quality). At the heart of project success projects: vision, trust, and collective commitment.

Nota Bene:

The contributors have drawn their inspiration from their professional life, each speaks only in his own name, and we would like to point out that none of the client companies or employers of the co-authors can be called into question by the content of this document.

The sketch notes and pictures illustrating this document have been created with the help of Microsoft Bing and the Generative AI tool provided by DALL-E from open.ai.

Finally, beyond the "Lab Hybrid" members who wrote content, we would like to thank all the people who contributed through their reviews, comments, or participation at different stages during our collective thinking within the "**Lab Hybrid**".

Here are their names in alphabetical order: Stéphane ABIVEN, Cécile ALLAIRE, Claudine BLANQUIER, Fabrice GILLET, Jérôme GUERS, Benoit GUILLET, Maixent HOUENOU-HOUNSINOU, Jean-Yves KLEIN, Cédric MATIONGO, Michel VERDUN.

With the publication of this manuscript, we are also happy to welcome Cécilia DOMRANE, for the animation of our community, and the continuation of this fabulous adventure.

Preface

As CEO of the Project Management Institute's global community, I am a privileged witness to the constant evolution of our profession and the need to adopt new approaches, overcome vain oppositions, and meet the challenges we face.

With this preface, I am pleased to introduce an initiative by the PMI France Chapter: a practical guide to hybrid project management. This represents an innovative and essential approach for our members.

Indeed, we are managing more and more projects in an uncertain world, and their complexity continues to increase. The question is not whether projects are carried out in a planned or agile way, but rather whether they are ultimately successful.

I am proud to support this initiative, which will contribute to the ongoing evolution of our profession. At PMI, we firmly believe that "Full Blend Project Management" is a crucial step towards improving our practices and ensuring that we achieve the results we expect.

I encourage you to explore the pages of this guide, and in particular the real-life situations presented, to learn from them and apply them to your own work. Whether you are a seasoned project management professional or just starting out, "Full Blend Project Management" has the potential to transform the way you manage projects.

However, this guide is only the first step in a collective effort to extend this initiative, enriched by new experiences and situations.

We need your help.

Enjoy reading it and come share your "Full Blend Projects"!

Pierre Le Manh, President and CEO of PMI WW
https://www.linkedin.com/in/pierre-le-manh-3a4158/

1

1. Fundamental principles

The Agile mode, historically linked to software development, is associated with information systems. So, what is its relevance beyond that, for manufacturing or the business?

The hybrid question was, therefore, originally essentially this: how to diffuse Agile in the traditional project world? How to have selection criteria to determine, at the portfolio level, the right method (Waterfall or Agile) for each of the projects that make up the portfolio. The question of mixing the two modes of hybridizing methods, tools, and techniques from the two worlds within a single project had not yet really been asked.

Opposing the two visions (Waterfall and Agile) is not relevant; they are complementary: making them converge, and combining them, has become an imperative.

The ability to master and mobilize the different approaches - Waterfall, Agile, Agile at scale, and Hybrid - is imperative. Upstream of projects, at the demand level, choosing the right approach is essential; within the same project, mixing the use of tools and techniques from the Waterfall and Agile modes and hybridizing is a major asset for achieving the expected benefits.

Convinced of the interest in adopting this new approach, we can illustrate it with models from the history of music: classical vs. jazz, the irruption of rock'n'roll, and what they can teach us in our project world in full transformation.

- Strengths and limits of Waterfall and Agile modes

Waterfall mode

In terms of vocabulary, the Waterfall mode can also be called V-cycle, W-cycle, classic, traditional, predictive, and planner.

By analogy, we can compare the Waterfall approach to a symphonic orchestra: 80 musicians, and one conductor. Each one has received solid musical training; they have a specific score corresponding to their respective role, for example, the first violin, the second cello, etc. There are no surprises for the audience nor for the musicians; the work announced before the concert will be played in strict accordance with the score and its indications. Most of the time, only the conductor and the orchestra are known by the audience.

This predictive approach is based on deductive reasoning. A deduction is an inference in which, if the premises are true, the conclusion is necessarily true. The deduction moves from the truth of the premises to the truth of the conclusion. The limit of this approach is that it can be mechanistic, sometimes even static, marked by a process culture, with defined inputs and outputs. Clearly, if, at the time of the initialization of the project, its scope is perfectly described and stable, we can deduce a detailed and reliable plan to implement it, including, for example, the establishment of an exhaustive work breakdown structure.

The difficulty we face in our project world is that the initial conditions (requirements, functionalities, objectives) can change throughout the project, which implies updating the scope and the project plan continuously. Unfortunately, the cumbersome nature of change management and the rigidity of the Waterfall approach do not always allow for dynamic updating. We are then victims of the famous tunnel effect.

For some projects, we need to use a global deductive approach so as not to be locked into the sole field of immediate experience; we need to understand and grasp them in their entirety as well as their dependencies and represent them precisely in an architectural way. This is typically one of the strengths of the classical project approach.

Finally, in the traditional project management approach, there is a project manager and controlling and very structured project governance.

Agile Mode

In terms of vocabulary, the Agile mode can be called empirical, adaptive, iterative, and incremental.

There are many Agile approaches, but they share the same set of values and principles (see "The Agile Manifesto for Software Development", published in February 2001). Agilists consider that Agile is not a method but a state of mind and a framework.

By analogy, we can compare the Agile approach to a modern jazz band, such as that of Miles DAVIS: the band is made up of three to eight musicians, each of whom is a virtuoso on his or her instrument. There are no more scores but chord grids. The grid provides a framework for musicians to have a common reference, especially for improvisation. The piece played, often a standard of popular music, leaves room for improvisation for each of the musicians who interact dynamically with each other and with the audience. The audience comes to listen to a group of musicians, where each one is known by the audience, and each evening the same piece can take different forms and get different "performances".

From the traditional point of view, we may believe, wrongly, that the original sin of the Agile mode is to come from software development and to concern only projects in information systems for small teams. However, this is not the real limit of this approach; answers have already been provided with Agile at scale. The diffusion of Agile in all sectors of activity demonstrates its effectiveness and its applicability outside of information systems.

The real limits of Agile are structural, and conceptual, with the philosophy that is at its source and nourishes it: empiricism.

Empiricism considers that knowledge is based on the accumulation of observations and measurable facts, from which we can extract general laws by inductive reasoning, thus going from the concrete to the abstract, sensible experience being the origin of all knowledge or belief.

Immanuel KANT, in _Critique of Pure Reason,_ gave thanks to David HUME, pillar of empiricism, for having awakened him from his "dogmatic sleep". Reason and formal logic alone cannot allow us to grasp reality in its entirety and complexity; the integration of experience is necessary to apprehend it effectively.

We can thank the Agile mode for having made us evolve in the management of our projects. However, if we want to build a product or run a project based on experience alone, trial and error, and blocks of increments, a large part of their reality can escape us, such as the portfolio dimension or dependencies with other projects, global or extrinsic risks.

Test/Fail and learn, a policy of small steps, iterations, production of increments, and induction, are, therefore, typical modalities of the Agile mode. They are very powerful in use; they allow to manage changes continuously and make the scope (Backlog) of the project/product evolve throughout its development. On the other hand, they do not respond to all the situations we have to face, in the complexity and diversity of the projects we carry out.

Agile has had very positive effects on the diffusion of new practices and techniques that were not "Agile" in themselves. However, they accompany its implementation, such as: managing by value, delivering value, engaging all stakeholders from the beginning of the project, co-designing, co-constructing, using visual management, applying the "enough design up-front" approach, etc. These practices can be integrated into the Waterfall mode, which is a specific form of hybridization.

Finally, especially in the Agile Scrum framework, there is no project manager but a Product Owner and a Scrum Master (a role called in other agile methods: Iteration Manager).

- ### Defining the hybridization mode

In our Waterfall-Agile dialectic, there is the central question of the vision of the organization, in particular: project mode versus product mode. Are these terms opposed? No, they are complementary. The product is the result; the project is the path. To succeed, the two are inseparable.

To illustrate this point, we can compare the hybrid mode to Rock'n'roll. Popular music, sometimes simple to play (such as the first songs of THE BEATLES), or complex (as with LED-ZEPPELIN), is accessible to the public and with a very high diffusion. The musicians don't have to be virtuosos or know how to read a score to play this music. The audience comes to listen to this group and not another, to hear their repertoire. The surprise effect is limited for the audience: in concert, they don't know the order of the pieces that will be played, but they know most of the songs and want to hear them. Improvisation, contrary to jazz, has little place in a rock concert, but the live show allows a certain freedom in the interpretation, its form, and its staging.

Most of the time, the group has the same "set list" of songs, which it plays in different venues during its tour.

Having established the principles, strengths, and limitations of the Waterfall and Agile approaches, we must now propose a new representation. This new representation does not confine and goes beyond the dualism that would oppose the two modes: induction-deduction, project-product, and old-modern.

Agile and Waterfall are not the only answer to the diversity of situations and projects that we must carry out.

Our answer is hybridization.

Hybridization is a generic term that designates a multiplicity and variability of situations.

How do we implement hybridization in our project world?

Understanding the strengths and limitations of each approach and mastering all the concepts, techniques, and tools they provide, we must know how to use each one wisely or combine them, depending on the nature of the work to be accomplished and its environment.

The share of one and the other can vary from 0 to 100% depending on the products and projects to be carried out and the situations. The same is true for the mobilization of tools and techniques from both modes.

As a reminder, in the PMBOK® Guide Seventh Edition, the hybridization concept is introduced at the level of the development approach: predictive, adaptive, and hybrid. The "tailoring" concept has a broader spectrum: development life cycle and approach, processes, commitment (of people), tools, techniques, artifacts, and, more generally, governance.

"There is no single approach to be applied to all projects at all times" – PMBOK® Guide Seventh Edition

- ## Hybridization Best Practices Guide

Our vision of the document: we want it to be simple, pragmatic, useful, and usable by as many people as possible. It is evolving and should be updated and enriched regularly. It contains eight specific situations to illustrate the diversity of hybrid practices. It is not self-supporting and requires the reader to have sufficient knowledge of Waterfall and Agile.

With hybridization, we propose new criteria of analysis, and new grids of understanding and decision, in the service of operational excellence. It is a matter of affirming our values and principles, building a framework, defining the rules of the game, and the methods of execution and deployment.

We have identified three axes as a reading grid to analyze the various hybridization situations: governance, methodological framework, and human dimension.

Indeed, hybridization is an approach that goes beyond the methodological framework that encourages the mixing of tools and practices. It is multi-dimensional and integrates governance and the human dimension of projects.

These three axes will be fed by eight situations to illustrate the benefits of hybridization: the problems encountered and how to respond to them. Why is the choice of a hybrid approach relevant? What tools or techniques from both worlds can be used, and in what ways?

Beyond the guide itself, **we wish to set up a community of practice for hybridization in projects** that support the acculturation and dissemination of this new approach by enriching it with feedback from members and by confronting it with reality.

Hybrid Governance

It includes:

- The organization, its culture, and maturity to implement hybridization.

- Hybrid portfolio management (end-to-end approach from request/initiative to execution).

- Decision support criteria to choose one of the different project approaches available (Waterfall, Agile, Scalable Agile, Hybrid...), or to mix them.

- Committee and governance processes/rituals in a hybrid environment.

- Management and monitoring of a hybrid portfolio (KPI and OKR).

The methodological framework of hybrid project management

It includes:

- Why and how to insert Agile techniques/rituals/tools within a Waterfall project, and according to which criteria and rules?

- Why and how to insert Waterfall techniques/processes/tools within an Agile project, and according to which criteria and rules?

- Why and how to mix Agile and Waterfall within the same project (end to end, in parallel, successively), and according to which criteria and rules?

- How to manage and synchronize Waterfall and Agile within the same project?

The human dimension in hybrid mode

It includes:

- Why and how to spread the values and organizational culture that support the hybrid approach?

- What mindset and attitude do we need to have to work in hybrid mode?

- Why and how to implement hybrid skills (training, coaching, mentoring, a community of practice, etc.)?

- What knowledge and skills are required to work in hybrid mode?

2. Situations

For us, the notion of situation designates a position and the choice of project stakeholders in a set of real data. To illustrate the diversity of situations in which hybridization responds to the challenges encountered, we are going to present eight concrete cases:

Situation A: I am required to manage my project in Waterfall, but I would like to use some good Agile practices without changing the project governance.

Situation B: Reconcile Waterfall and Agile in the same project, or how to support the team to work with a hybrid approach?

Situation C: My client cannot wait to see the final deliverable on his project. How can I evolve my Waterfall project organization to have more regular deliveries by integrating the iterative approach of Agile mode?

Situation D: My Agile project never ends, or I add sprints indefinitely!

Situation E: How to manage a portfolio that includes Agile, Waterfall, and Hybrid projects?

Situation F: Top management imposes on me a reporting and governance that seem incompatible with my management in Agile.

Situation G: I must start a project in Agile, but I am not convinced that this is the right method. Could the hybridization approach help me?

Situation H: How can Critical Chain avoid delays for a solution consisting of sub-projects executed in parallel in Waterfall and Agile?

The structuring elements that guided the description of each situation are as follows:

- Context
- Governance
- Methodological framework
- Human dimension
- Success story/conclusion

Situation A: I am required to manage my project in Waterfall, but I would like to use some good Agile practices without changing the project governance.

- ## Context

My company responds to a call for tenders financed by the client for the construction of an industrial infrastructure of several hundred million euros. I have one year to build a technical and financially binding offer over several years.

My team is young, and some members have just experienced a difficult project managed in Waterfall. I must adapt the Waterfall execution model of the project to design an innovative solution while developing the motivation of the team.

Lessons Learnt meetings bringing together stakeholders (those still present after three years of the project) have demonstrated their ineffectiveness. Information is difficult to find, and some meetings sometimes turn into a settling of accounts between departments, and the resulting action plans are not followed.

In recent years, the evolution of the market has forced our industrial society to rethink its organization. In particular, the arrival of smaller, more agile structures capable of bringing a product to market in record time, where we needed 5 to 10 years.

Our activities were too sequential, and the business lines did not always have the same level of information on the status of the various developments in our activities. An external audit recommended that we set up a cross-functional management structure for our projects to allow a shared vision of the progress of the portfolio of our various projects.

For several years now, new product development projects have been carried out within a hybrid framework.

- ## Governance

According to the stages of the project, to integrate agility into our Waterfall execution:

At initiation phase

- I mobilize an Agile coach to help me put in place the required collective dynamics.

At planning phase

- My project governance is facilitated via ad-hoc meetings (releases/functions) by optimizing the choice of participants in project meetings, daily meetings, or Steering Committees. This governance is supported by a dedicated project space (physical or virtual project room) to allow animation in visual management (board, wall, etc.).

- I use Agile rituals to facilitate problem-solving, at the right level of the project organization.

At execution phase

- I continue reporting and reviews with management, as required by my company's framework. The Waterfall comitology remains in place. However, I raise awareness of new practices with the aim of avoiding any residual double reporting.

At closing phase

- Lessons Learnt meetings, inspired by Agile mode retrospectives, are more frequent throughout the project and in the end, more constructive and more pleasant.

- ## Methodological framework

According to the stages of the project, to integrate agility into our Waterfall execution:

At initiation phase

- I build a project space with all the physical and IT tools to allow information to be gathered in the same place and to organize collective activities. This room can also be virtual.

At planning phase

- I give more room to progressive elaboration (**rolling wave planning**).

- I am inspired by the Agile ceremony of "**product backlog refinement**" to boost change management with the establishment of a dedicated committee and aim for shared responsibility.

- I introduce the notions of Minimum Viable Product (MVP) and "Test & Learn" on the definition of the scope of the project: for example, I set up "**value engineering**" workshops to define, in a short period of time, a preliminary solution at optimized cost which will serve as a basis for the development of the technical file, the development of the execution plan, and the costing of the binding offer.

- I decide that a "Work Package (WP)", a component or a sub-project, will be managed in agility.

At execution phase

- I establish a culture of feedback, and I plan intermediate demonstrations with the beneficiaries concerned within my project to confront my current product in progress with their expectations: Proof of Concept (POC), prototype, pilot, beta test, etc.

At closing phase

- I carry out the synthesis of what has been collected continuously (using, for example, the assessments of previous retrospectives or a list of problems and changes).

- I propose intermediate acceptance tests to deliver value as we go along without waiting for the overall delivery of the project.

- ## Human dimension

According to the stages of the project, to integrate agility into our Waterfall execution:

At planning phase

- I federate an agile collective to create a purpose and illustrate the challenges of the project in a different way.

- I strive to understand the different personalities that make up my team (i.e., DISC, MBTI, Insight, Process Com, etc.) to get to know each other better and understand the context of the project, considering individual and collective profiles.

- I collaboratively develop the objectives of the project, including objectives related to the development of the team, and objectives related to the long-term strategy of my company, in addition to QHSE objectives (for example) and traditional "cost" and "time" objectives.

- I use collective intelligence and cooperation to control risks and define key milestones in the project life cycle.

At execution phase

- I establish a culture of feedback, and I plan regular retrospectives with my team to take stock of the organization of the project. I feed the feedback over time.

At closing phase

- I put in place a "gratitude" system, financial rewards for objectives achieved, and qualitative rewards towards involved employees (knowing how to say thank you and highlighting the work accomplished and the successes).

- I document feedback on the project in a knowledge base to benefit the organization and future projects.

All along the project life cycle

- I make sure that the operational organization of the project and the rituals place the collaborators at the heart of the projects so that they can intervene at any time to report a risk or a blockage or to give a progress report of their work.

- I am inspired by the "serious games" approach (quizzes, challenges) to convey the main messages.

- I put in place a regular assessment of the well-being of the teams, which is monitored with a specific dashboard (inspired by the famous *"mood marble"* or another ROTI technique...).

- When teams are working mostly virtually, I set up the "daily alignment meeting" routine.

- I celebrate each key "milestone" achieved and recognize everyone's performance.

- Success story

The execution of my project, aiming to infuse hybridization, made it possible to deliver a solution adapted to the constraints of the market with increased productivity while changing the initial scope. It made it possible to maintain the motivation of the teams throughout the execution by reinforcing the feeling of belonging and accountability.

It also met the expectations of young employees by offering them a more collaborative and human-centered management style. This hybridization mode of execution has generated interest from peers. Finally, numerous feedbacks shared within the organization have made it possible to consider areas for improvement.

Situation B: Reconcile Waterfall and Agile in the same project, or how to support the team to work with a hybrid approach?

- **Context**

For seven years, new product development projects have been carried out in a hybrid framework. The backbone of the project methodology in the organization is, first, predictive, inherent to industrial environments, with a succession of milestones that will transcribe the maturity of product development and our ability to manufacture them.

However, we also have a strong software dimension in our systems to control our electronics. Software development is mainly done following the Agile (Scrum) approach.

The company that develops IT solutions have chosen to organize work with teams operating in agile mode for the presentation layer (front office) and teams in Waterfall to manage asynchronous processing (back office and data volume).

The company starts the construction of a project of several million euros. This project includes various lots whose specifications are detailed and based on numerous industrial references. These will be executed in Waterfall. However, one of the lots is technological innovation. This requires many interactions with customers to define needs and understand the associated constraints. Could hybridization help?

- **Governance**

How to define the project governance?

- I build a mixed team in key cross-functional areas.

- I set up collaborative tools for both types of teams (for example MS Teams, iObeya platform, Atlassian suite, etc.).

- I combine the two approaches with integration milestones: 8 to 10 milestones per project, spaced two to three months apart. They make it possible to visualize the progress of developments and thus reduce the tunnel effect.

- I redefine the Waterfall processes to integrate Agile and allow synchronization.

- I integrate Waterfall requirements (security, work environment, configuration management, etc. i.e., the technical constraints of the order of requirements more than functionalities) in the product backlog.

- I ensure flexibility, and highlight the choices of the Product Owner and the teams, with the implementation of a reporting and decision cycle, centered on the content of the backlog to be reviewed (the "backlog refinement" ceremony)

- I quickly disseminate project and program information: implementation of an effective reporting system, with a project summary on the one hand (success, blockages, risks), and a network of meetings ranging from the project meeting / Daily Scrum to the Steering Committee.

- ### Methodological framework

An evaluation grid makes it possible to confirm the possibility of executing the new "work package" (WP) in agility and with what level of prerequisites.

I define the criteria of the evaluation grid with questions – for example:

- Am I able to frame the content of this WP?

- Do I know how to predict the expected result?

- Is it possible to deliver a minimal autonomous version, which can be improved by successive iterations? (Minimum Viable Product – MVP)

- Does the expected content of this WP depend on other uncertain factors in the project?

- Are the beneficiaries of this WP well-identified, and are they available to participate in agile governance?

- Can I limit the perimeter of this WP so that it does not encroach on the others?

- At each new phase of the WP, the question may arise. It may be desirable to return to Waterfall mode for this WP, if relevant.

How to integrate the human side, the points of view of the stakeholders, the acculturation, and the management of the change?

In the case of an isolated Agile WP in a Waterfall project, it would remain an exception (weak hybridization approach). This may cause a cultural shock and then reluctance from some stakeholders. Consequently, we did the following:

- Communicate with the stakeholders impacted by this WP on the singularities of agility: iterations, incremental deliveries, the definition of content as you go, stronger mobilization of users, etc.

- Help team members contributing to agile WP to adopt hybridization.

- Deploy dedicated training to support change at the individual level.

- Accompany the change at the collective level with a facilitator mastering hybridization (coach profile) who helped us to ensure the interface with the other WPs and good communication between the teams.

The framework as such created puts employees at the heart of the projects as they can intervene at any time to report a risk or a blockage to give a progress report of their work.

By becoming "Product Owner" over the entire duration (or part of it) of the project, the Project Manager or WP leader may have **feared losing control and authority** over his team.

However, he was also able to value the benefits of better communicating with his external client and internal clients. He better prioritized the rest of the Product Backlog and **maximize value creation for customer satisfaction**.

A telecom integrator provides a set of complex communications solutions to its client. Client and supplier usually work in Waterfall. This mode is suitable for this type of project requiring integration of equipment in the data center, engineering, hardware configuration, middleware, and then deployment on the operator's capillary network.

During a new contract for an innovative solution, an important software component was not framed. It is a transverse supervision brick with very wide possibilities. The client identifies certain needs but is unable to limit them. He wants to integrate multiple functionalities while measuring the complexity of the solution to be implemented. The subject becomes contentious.

We have therefore returned to the fundamentals of the Agile approach: collaboration with the client. The integrator offers his client to carry out this Work Package in Agile mode with a limited number of sprints, the creation of a product backlog, and the creation of "User Stories" with their prioritization by users.

This approach made it possible to get out of an impasse, met the expectations of the customer, and restored value to the project management by the integrator.

Situation C: My client cannot wait to see the final deliverable on his project. How can I evolve my Waterfall project organization to have more regular deliveries by integrating the iterative approach of Agile mode?

- Context

We are in the design phase of a project managed in Waterfall mode. The client wishes to deploy a new payroll and time management software for all its employees. This new software will replace its old tool, which can no longer follow legal developments. All employees are made up of diverse populations with specific needs. This requires designing and implementing many features specific to each population, and the risk is high of not correctly understanding the needs.

Noting a gap between needs and functionalities to be tested at the time of the acceptance phase would have a direct impact on the production start date of the project, which the customer cannot afford. It is imperative that teams test the application quickly.

During the first steering committee, after the start of the design phase, the client tells us that he wishes to avoid the tunnel effect during the production phase (between the end of the design and the start of the UAT phase).

- Governance

To meet the need to reduce the tunnel effect, we have organized a **dedicated project committee with functional referents and project managers**. The solution proposed by this dedicated project committee was presented to the steering committee for validation.

The purpose of the dedicated project committee is to:

- Finalize the design phase and obtain the validation of the client for the functional specifications of the project.

- Merge the production phase (configuration and development) with the acceptance phase. We have named this new phase "*expanded UAT phase*".

- Define the functional releases that can - in the expanded acceptance phase - be delivered while minimizing the impacts both in terms of cost and project time:

  o The validation of the impacts is done by the steering committee, which follows the project committee.

- Identify the milestones for each functional release delivery: a first one is set one month after the validation of the design phase. A period of 3 to 4 weeks between each delivery until complete delivery to the customer (duration four months).

  o Starting with the second release, **all the estimated effort of each release must be lower than the capacity of the project team**: the objective is <u>to add to the scope of the current</u> batch the bug fixing of the previous releases.

- Define the bug-fixing rules. The team that develops the next release is the same team that fixes bugs from previous releases, and priorities should always be clear.

We have adapted the organization and agenda of the project committees during the expanded UAT phase:

- A project committee per week to validate the accuracy of the application released compared to the target application.

- All the key people, both on the integrator side and on the customer side, attend and participate in these committees when their knowledge is necessary to decide or arbitrate during the meeting (if applicable).

- Defects are classified as business-critical or non-business-critical.

- The impacts of business-critical bugs (when any) are validated or escalated to the members of the steering committee.

- We discuss the latest identified defects and validate their relevance (sometimes it was not a bug, but a misunderstanding of the client on the functionality).

- The client is informed of the corrections made and those planned with the next release. The questions of the project teams are dealt with as they arise.

- • Methodological framework

In parallel with the delivery of each release, we organized a presentation of the functionalities delivered to the teams in charge of the UAT. This presentation allowed the teams to be trained on the functionalities to be tested. In addition, we have implemented a rigorous defect management process with two types of anomalies:

- **Business-critical:** bugs impacting one or more functionalities planned in the next releases and to be corrected asap, together with the build of the next release. Before starting the correction:

  o The proposed solution must be validated with the customer's business team to ensure that there is no new misunderstanding.

  o The impacts of the solution (cost, time, business value) are validated by the project committee and, if necessary, be escalated to an extraordinary steering committee.

  o The client team in charge of the UAT (user acceptance tests) phase must update its test books by adding the test of the business-critical defects which have been corrected.

- **Non-Business-critical:** bugs fixed when the team becomes available.

  o Their correction must not impact the delivery of the next release.

  o The priority of these anomalies (blocking, major or minor) will begin to apply from the delivery of the last functional release.

  o The client team in charge of acceptance plans the validation of these anomalies according to their availability and after having validated the new functionalities of the latest release delivered.

- Human dimension

The implementation of this hybrid methodology required some adjustments on both sides.

Integrator:

- Adapt the planning of the teams by facilitating the simultaneous work of the technical team (in charge of configuration/development) and the functional team (in charge of explaining the design).

- Functional teams carry out unit testing as internal releases are made to avoid delays and provide continuous feedback.

Client:

- Mobilize the client's business teams throughout the expanded UAT phase.

- The objective is:

  o Exchange regularly with the integrator's teams and guide them in their choice of settings/development.

  o To make themselves available to participate in presentations/training organized by the integrator each time a new release is delivered.

  o To start and carry out the UAT tests several months before the date planned at the start of the project.

- Conclusion

Constraints

- The integrator had to strengthen the project team and increase project management costs.

- The client had to strengthen its team to ensure that all their tasks were done during the expanded UAT phase.

The benefits for the customer

- Validate at an early stage of the project that the functionalities released corresponds to its requirements (strong reduction of the tunnel effect).

- Detect and fix misunderstandings very quickly.

- Complete the requirements given during the design phase.

- Respect the go-live date of the application (strong client constraint).

Thus, the life cycle initially planned for the implementation of this project has been adapted. A "tailor-made" approach between the integrator and the client has made it possible to meet project requirements and constraints.

Situation D: My Agile project never ends, or I add sprints indefinitely!

• Context

In Agile mode, the development team is stable over the duration of the project, so the budget allocated to human resources is also stable over the duration and thus predictable and controlled, if the duration of the project is set and respected. The temptation is great to add new features to the product backlog as the project progresses, even if the next sprints are already filled. In this case, it seems logical to add new sprints indefinitely and insert new user stories (US) within the product backlog.

We quickly find ourselves faced with the paradox of the *infinite hotel*. We can always add user stories (US) to the product backlog produced from the top, from the bottom, in distant sprints, as in the next sprints, by de-prioritizing some US to prioritize the most recent...

The danger in using an Agile approach is never to finish.

• Governance

If we are constrained by time and resources and add sprints indefinitely, hybrid governance of the project should be put in place.

Are we in a project with a defined beginning and end? If so, how do we get out of it?

• Methodological framework

Several cases in this "infinite hotel" situation are possible (and the list is not exhaustive):

- The Agile team, to implement certain functionalities or user stories, has as a prerequisite the delivery by other teams of certain components, which, themselves, are never finished.
  - o If most interdependent projects are in Agile mode, then agility at scale or a hybrid approach should be implemented.

- If this Agile project is isolated in a Waterfall environment, then it seems appropriate to adopt the governance mentioned in situation B.
- Project increments are constantly rejected, the quality is poor, and the deliverables contain blocking issues preventing their validation (quality issues).
- Project increments are accepted but with reserve. However, these extensions are accepted because the Agile team is in place, and extensions are added to the product backlog (problem with the method of building the backlog and its prioritization).

Value creation is not enough to align needs and finalize execution. The risk of drift is great, and knowing how to work in Agile mode requires significant organizational maturity and discipline.

It may then be necessary to come up with a hybrid project approach and use the Waterfall vision lens to step back:

- Rethink the end of a project with a cost/time/ambition balance (replacing the content).
- Build a "pseudo" Work Breakdown Structure based on ambitions to redefine a target framework. We can rely on the WBS to review the decomposition of epics, features, and other user stories.
- Establish milestones and/or gates.
- Set up a steering committee to validate and monitor ambitions and strategic changes.
- Qualify more precisely the requirements that are the source of the current backlog (e.g., MosCoW).

- Human dimension

A team in distress is the result of the extreme delays experienced by the project in Agile mode that never ends. This is a warning sign that should prompt us to initiate the process mentioned here.

The longer the duration of the project, the more the question of skills is emphasized: a high level of maturity and rigor in the execution of the Agile framework (cf. Definition of Ready, Definition of Done) is imperative. Training all project stakeholders in Agile and respecting the approach is essential to protect ourselves from the "infinite hotel".

- Conclusion

In this situation often encountered, the Agile mode must be enriched: by a very solid product vision defined as soon as needs arise by hybridization that gives greater control of the scope of the project and its requirements. Hybridization, by setting from the outset of the project the rules of the game, temporal, and budgetary limits, as well as Tollgates of synchronization, allows us to avoid the trap of "never finished" in Agile.

Situation E: How to manage a portfolio that includes projects in Agile mode, in Waterfall mode, and Hybrid projects?

- ### Context

The Board of Directors, in agreement with management and taking into account market aspects and business objectives, defines the overall vision and strategy To meet and achieve organizational goals; portfolios are constructed and implemented.

They bring together and coordinate all activities: programs, projects, products, and even operations.

In essence, a portfolio is characterized by the following:

- Its transversality
- The nature of the programs and projects that make it up.
- Its governance structure.
- The stakeholders.
- A control tower to guarantee that management and prioritization rules are applied.
- The degree of progress of the various programs and projects in their life cycle, tracked by a dashboard and indicators.

Hybridization goes beyond the methodological framework and is also part of the portfolio management approach.

The portfolio is the translation and operational expression of the company's strategy.

In this context, the annual plans are reviewed according to the company's updated strategic choices, which will define and prioritize the components of the portfolio.

To achieve tangible results, we recommend a hybrid portfolio since it considers the plurality of situations, projects, and their management methods. Delivering the value expected by clients, first and foremost members of top management including sponsors and business units, is an imperative and requires nuance, i.e., responding in a relevant way to their different needs and requirements. This implies a dynamic portfolio management that integrates the different available methods, as well as synchronizing and consolidating them.

The portfolio is multi-dimensional. Its life cycle can be influenced by the links between the different projects, the maturity of the organization, and the availability of its resources.

Managing a portfolio involves:

- Characterize its constituent elements.
- Assess the capacity of the organization to absorb the workload.
- Ensure visibility and alignment with strategic direction.
- Identify the parameters to be monitored, establish, and animate the relevant dashboards.
- Prioritize and make decisions.
- Manage the budgets relating to the portfolio and adapt them if necessary.

The portfolio manager must rely on these elements to make decisions, optimize resources, and achieve the strategic objectives of the company.

According to our three axes of analysis which are governance, the methodological framework, and the human dimension, here are our suggestions for managing a hybrid portfolio.

- ## Governance

Project portfolios can be managed by a single entity in the organization or under the direction of several entities. In one case, governance is generally at the head of this department (Finance, IT, HR). In the other, transversality will be preponderant with the existence of a PMO (Project Management Office) or a VMO (Value Management Office).

In both cases, governance ensures a good understanding of the expected value. The commitment of the General Management is crucial.

Governance must ensure the ability of organizations to carry out projects, i.e., to know the number of projects that can be managed together at a given time. To manage the portfolio, she needs visibility on each program and project. A dashboard is drawn up to give a synthetic and understandable picture of the portfolio's situation, indicating, among other things, progress, resources consumption, deadlines, risks and impacts, **Time to Market**, KPIs, or OKRs. This involves sharing a common project language, regardless of the project management modality used.

Portfolio management guarantees the strategic alignment of its constituent elements and prioritizes them by **clarifying the decision criteria**:

- Arbitration consists of defining priorities during an integration point with stakeholders and reallocating resources, often at the expense of lower-priority projects.
- Focusing consists in putting a point of attention on the projects/programs requiring it; a fever chart can be used to map the degrees of advancement.
- Decision-making is centered on the value and performance of the project.
- The characteristics of the different projects make it possible to determine the type of governance to adopt.

Furthermore, the financial management of a hybrid portfolio requires comparable data. This may involve, for example, transforming the costs (in points) of Agile teams into men/days to make them comparable to the workloads (in days) of Waterfall teams.

Hybrid portfolio governance requires strong adaptability from its pilot.

- Methodological framework

It is recommended that the portfolio manager and the managers of the various projects jointly determine the management methods in Waterfall, Agile, or hybrid as soon as possible. The conditions for exercising the execution methods during the life cycle of a hybrid project are thus clarified and decided based on a shared reading grid. Within a hybrid project, key stakeholders have knowledge of how to manage the transition, its impacts, and its consequences.

To observe and anticipate changes in the portfolio or even to warn if a project is no longer under control, regular portfolio reviews must be set up in advance, co-constructed with the key stakeholders, at just the right frequency so as not to disrupt team operations. This ensures that reporting is comparable. The person in charge of the portfolio leads them, with the managers of the various programs and projects. Ideally, decisions on critical items are made during these events. **Depending on the level of maturity of the organizations,** the monitoring reports can be dynamic and updated on a collaborative tool in real-time.

The portfolio manager cannot impose standard indicators for everyone. It is all the key stakeholders who agree on the KPIs and OKRs, to design the portfolio dashboard. Usual management indicators – quality, cost, lead time, risk analysis, ROI, NPV, etc. – are used to dynamically observe and anticipate changes in the portfolio.

Visual management tools are adapted to this use and chosen for monitoring and alerts. Beyond the common indicators, the teams remain free in their organization.

Communication rules are established in advance in terms of reporting from project managers to stakeholders.

- Human dimension

The motivation and involvement of stakeholders are affected by a unilateral decision of the mode of project management determined by the portfolio manager, who is familiar with the different methodologies without dogmatic preconceptions. He is vigilant about the meaning of the words, expressions, and concepts used to understand and be understood by all.

The portfolio manager is flexible enough to obtain the right information, to be able to interact regardless of the project's mode of operation, ensures transparency, and demonstrates adaptability to the different project universes (Waterfall, Agile, Hybrid), depending on the pace of work of each. He ensures that the resources common to the different projects speak the same vocabulary and that they can understand each other.

Ideally, the portfolio pilot has the matrices of versatility and poly-skills of the resources of the organization or even of all the key stakeholders.

This cartography:

- Provides information on the teams' abilities to manage projects in different methods.
- Enables the implementation of training actions to broaden horizons on other project management methodologies.
- Enables us to identify resources most suited to hybrid mode operation, and position them in different configurations to develop team methods and rituals and enhance the organization's maturity (mentoring/coaching).

Resources are limited. Overloading them has an impact on serenity and efficiency. To avoid saturating them, it is important to identify limiting factors and hybrid skills as part of portfolio management.

The criteria and rules for prioritization, and alignment with strategic objectives must be understood by all to prevent the risk of frustration among teams upset by a cancellation or postponement by specifying that the decision is not correlated to the intrinsic performance of members of these teams but to a coordination decision.

- Success story

We acted as PMO Director for a portfolio of information systems transformation projects: approximately 300 concurrent projects organized into five functional areas; some managed within multi-year transformation programs.

The same pool of skills and resources was budgeted annually to serve these projects. The projects were in different phases, and some not initially identified were added after the budget review for strategic reasons.

The projects and programs in the portfolio were mainly conducted in Waterfall. However, many initiatives were conducted in Agile (cf., launching a prototype, developing an alternative solution to circumvent a technical constraint, etc.). Thus, this portfolio became a hybrid, and we needed to be able to arbitrate between activities carried out in Agile and projects in Waterfall, specifically to make resource allocation decisions.

Delivery (cutover in production mode) often occurs on weekends; we had set up a weekly management system for resource allocation with arbitration every Friday morning. The decisions taken were communicated (impact analysis) and could be modified until the following Friday morning. According to the trade-offs proposed to optimize immediate execution, the constraints were validated by Business leaders with shared visibility. Thus, regardless of the project management mode (plan based or agile), our portfolio arbitrations were set on the shortest time frame (7 rolling days, the following week).

It helped us to work better together. The key success factors were to impose 1) agility on Waterfall projects (absorption of changes from one week to the next); and 2) clients (project stakeholders at the governance level: managers and, if necessary, heads of functional entities) to get involved in decision-making at the portfolio management level.

Situation F: Top management imposes on me the responsibility for reporting and governance that seems incompatible with my management in Agile.

- ## Context

My company, a highly regulated industry, wants to release an innovative and disruptive product by a given date and a fixed budget. The needs are clear, but how to achieve them is uncertain. Corporate governance remains traditionally Waterfall, but I want to manage my project in Agile mode and use the associated techniques and tools daily.

How to meet the traditional requirements of top management and manage my project in Agile mode?

To answer this problem, here are the steps followed for a hybrid approach:

1. The initial needs expressed by the client and the key stakeholders of the project must be expressed in the form of macro-functions within a roadmap.

2. The non-negotiable constraints or requirements of these macro-functions must be identified, validated, and prioritized: standards, requirements, technologies, maturity and mentality of the organization and stakeholders, the requirement for innovation vs. competition, etc. Please note that the framework must be sufficiently precise but remain at a high level. This step corresponds to the DoR (Definition of Ready) of the macro-functions.

3. These macro functions must be prioritized and validated in a product backlog.

4. The teams in charge of carrying out the project agree on the delivery dates of the macro-functions, but they are free and responsible for the detailed content and the technical means to carry out each of the macro-functions.

5. From the start of the project, the planning of synchronization of Tollgates that are binding and regular, aligned with the project roadmap, is necessary. By analogy with a rally raid and its mandatory checkpoints, they will constitute the backbone of the project in terms of governance and management. These tollgates are sufficiently spaced out (depending on the project and its macro-functions) to determine the

34

status of the macro-functions to be performed. They are binding and non-negotiable points of passage. During these tollgates' reviews, a certain number of points will be systematically reviewed (KPI / OKR, spent budget, delivered value, identified risks, new need / obsolete need, need for resources, the possibility of outsourcing macro-functions, etc.)

6. Between each tollgate, the teams work in Agile mode and have full latitude to distribute the workload of the macro-functions to be carried out according to priorities (self-organization). For example, if the tollgates take place every three months, this allows Scrum mode to do 3 to 6 sprints (two to four weeks each) between each tollgate.

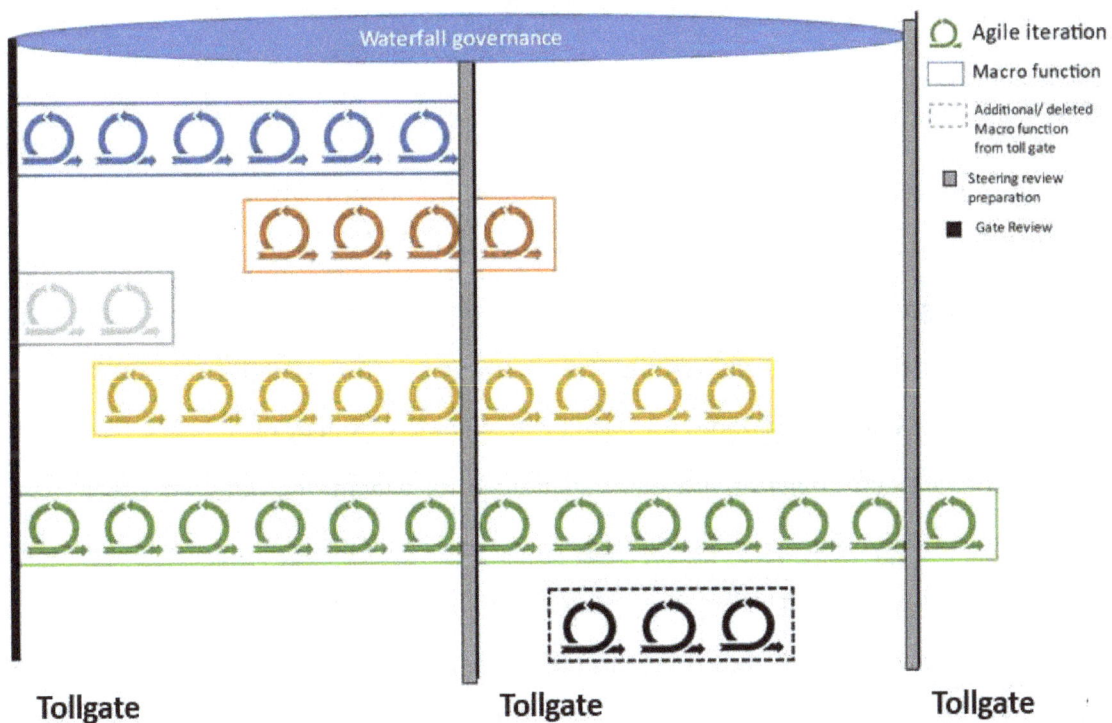

Governance Waterfall with Agile execution

According to our three axes of analysis: governance, methodological framework, and human dimension, here are our proposals to manage this situation:

- ## Governance

In our case, the governance is traditional and wants to set up strict control of the costs, deadlines, and risks of the project.

To make classic governance and Agile project management compatible, key stakeholders must be aligned before project execution, on the vision, roadmap, and macro-functions of the project (scope) to be carried out.

The tollgate is a mandatory synchronization point whose KPIs and OKRs, associated with the expected value of the project, have been defined in advance.

Management does not control the project in Agile mode, so it expects the following elements during these tollgates' reviews: budget spent, remaining to be done, status on macro-functions, synchronization, status on the value created, risks, etc.

- ## Methodological framework

To hybridize classic governance with an Agile mode, it is important to define macro-functions precisely and in a stable manner throughout the project.

You must be aligned with the level of granularity that characterizes these macro-functions. All stakeholders must determine the criteria that characterize the expected value and the state of "finished" (DoD: Definition of Done) for each of these macro-functions.

To frame the project, Tollgates are planned before its execution. Detailed checklists for the tollgate reviews will be defined beforehand, in agreement with the key stakeholders, and the elements constituting them will not be negotiable. The number of tollgates depends on the project itself, in particular, its duration, complexity, and challenges.

Regular retrospectives, as well as iteration reviews, will also help to avoid the tunnel effect between each tollgate.

- ## Human dimension

Project teams in Agile mode work with constant and defined resources.

They are free, between each "Tollgate," to organize and manage their work as they see fit. Project increment reviews must be kept ensuring alignment with needs. The Agile culture of transparency, inspection, and adaptation allows feedback loops (Sprint review, retrospective, technical debt review, etc.), avoiding misunderstandings and facilitating inclusion within teams.

- Conclusion

It is essential to have agreed on a common language, a shared vision, and the rules of the game from the start of the project. The hybridization with Waterfall governance and teams operating in Agile allows greater freedom and creativity of the teams (detailed content, technological means) and regular alignment with sponsors, which avoids the tunnel effect and allows regular adjustments. This approach allows you to focus on the value to be delivered, with enough freedom for trial and error or adjustment between each "Tollgate" while respecting budget and deadline requirements.

Situation G: I must start a project in Agile, but I am not convinced that this is the right method. Could the hybridization approach help me?

- **Context**

I am a software publisher in the field of machine security. This company operates in the industrial world and manages automation and industrial electrical projects.

The size of the company, and the diversity of the projects it conducts, produce complexity and disconnections:

- Between the strategy and the portfolio of projects/products
- Within the teams, due to the difficulty of finding and maintaining a sustainable production rhythm of User Stories (large size and complexity of epics)

Moreover, the actors in charge of the projects lack vision, and the teams lose cohesion.

Some characteristics of these difficulties:

- A practice of agility, but **not aligned with the Agile framework**: teams think they work in Agile mode, but their practices do not respect the fundamentals of agility (roles and responsibilities, artifacts, events, rituals, etc.).

- A mindset that must evolve to integrate a better consideration of the expectations of the development team (principle of the self-organized and autonomous team).

- Some projects must be part of a program: a set of interrelated projects, though a given project team does not know nor consider its dependencies with other projects.

- Project management is not adapted to the different phases of the project life cycle.

- The **project life cycle is not adjusted** to the constraints related to the complexity and size of the project organization: project management processes lack "scalability" and versatility. Processes are not scalable or versatile.

- A need for a decision grid to choose the right method (Waterfall, Agile, Hybrid): create a decision-making tool for managing possible options based on the different arbitration criteria.

- The need to rethink the effectiveness of the existing project processes:

    o The steering mode with the integration of visual project management; and

    o The contribution of hybridization as a response to increasingly complex project management (deliverable/product).

In a hybrid approach, multiple options are available to us.

- Governance

<u>Some hybrid governance principles:</u>

- Clarify this hybrid management mode: accept reality and recognize that we do neither agile nor plan ("plan based").

- Redefine the competency model (roles and responsibilities on the project) to improve performance and avoid confusion among actors.

- Bring together all projects, regardless of the method used, within a single portfolio.

- Structure the steering committee: members decide on the project methodology to be used according to the different selection criteria for the project in its environment. They ensure the project is carried out according to the chosen method. This implies that they know and know how to apply different methods.

- Methodological framework

Examples of criteria to consider:

- Risk management
- Lifecycle adjustment (Waterfall, Agile, Agile to Scale, Hybrid)
- Solution architecture analysis
- Execution and management
- ...

to be able to **define the selection grid appropriate to the project context and the organization and environment** in which it takes place.

⇨ Example of a guidance and decision grid:

Criteria	• Compulsory budgetary management and control • Risk management • Clear, precise, defined scope	• Content flexibility • Exploration • Relaunching a dynamic in an ongoing project • Value maximization	• Flexibility and pace variability • Complexity • Multi-business • Multiple dependencies • Multi-method • Technical / legal / compliance obligations • Value maximization • Risk management
Type of project	Mastered, known ⬇	Innovative ⬇	Complex ⬇
	Waterfall	**Agile, Agile at scale**	**Hybridization approach**

- Human dimension

Example of vigilance points:

- I reconnect the team's commitment to the objectives of the project, ensuring the variability of features production rhythms (avoiding unsustainable and continuous velocity).

- I optimize the workload and find a balance between the pull flow (Agile) and the push flow (Waterfall), depending on the team's capacity.

- I change the mindset and behavior of the team members: support the understanding of the principles of agility and integrate the values.
- I clarify the methodological choice that claims Agile but whose process management is entirely Waterfall.
- I define with the customer and stakeholders of the project ecosystem how to work.
- I align from the start with the customer, the end users, on the project management mode and the rules of the game.
- I specify the roles and responsibilities within the same project and, more broadly, at the level of the organization: project manager, product owner, scrum master, product leader, and project leader.
- I promote the development of sufficient knowledge areas and skills to evolve in a hybrid world, which requires training and coaching effort to master them.

- ## Conclusion

The hybridization approach must be implemented at the global level of the organization, with an end-to-end vision, to ensure operational excellence.

The essential prerequisite of hybridization is to know Waterfall and Agile properly and to understand their strengths and limitations. The failures encountered in our projects during the implementation of either approach are often related to the failure to respect the fundamentals of each of them: processes, rituals, artifacts, roles, and responsibilities... Hybridization is not a degraded project mode combining these two approaches. It is, on the contrary **a dynamic and controlled synthesis of the two methods** in order to deliver the expected value in costs and deadlines.

Situation H: How can Critical Chain avoid delays for a solution consisting of sub-projects executed in parallel in Waterfall and Agile?

- **Context**

This situation is treated theoretically without referring to a real case.

What is the Critical Chain?

A critical Chain is a tool to manage the project. It emphasizes securities of the schedule to create a common buffer in time and to manage project progress according to buffer consumption.

The key indicator in Critical Chain is the "Fever Chart", a project temperature graph that dynamically measures the progress ratio of the project's critical tasks execution and buffers time consumption needed to protect against uncertainties.

- **Governance**

Management by flows

- In "Waterfall" tasks are pushed according to execution logic
- In Agile, tasks are pulled in a progressive development process.
- In hybridization mode, these two approaches are reconciled by focusing on flow.

With the Critical Chain method, we measure the progress against what is "still to be done to finish", the Estimate To Complete (ETC), which is as estimated in the execution phase. This frees us from estimation errors when scheduling, that is to say: at a time when we do not really know the scope of the task in terms of functionalities, deadlines, available resources, allocated resources, and difficulties that appear in execution.

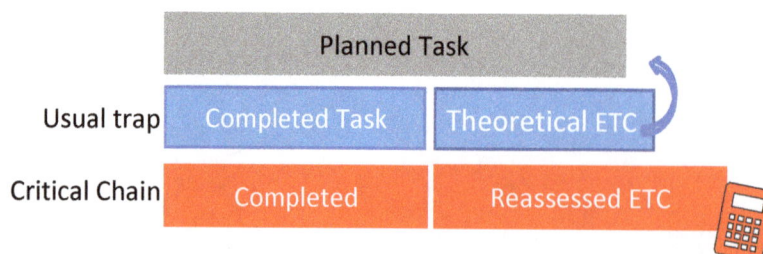

42

Integration point: the buffer

Let's imagine that the two chains of the project schedule need a synchronization point because of content logic on subsets deliverables: each subset estimates its effort duration for delivery perspectives (according to the expected achievement).

The corresponding network may look like the diagram below.

We can therefore imagine a common measure to manage the relative progress of both parties (the activities in the "Waterfall" method and those in the Agile method) of the same project. This results in a **mutualization of homogeneous buffers**.

Illustration of possible Integration points

If the critical path (shown in red in the diagram below) is positioned on the project part that is in the "Waterfall" method, a common buffer covers the longest chain. To keep the critical path as stable as possible, that is, to prevent secondary paths from becoming critical, a second buffer is added to each secondary chain.

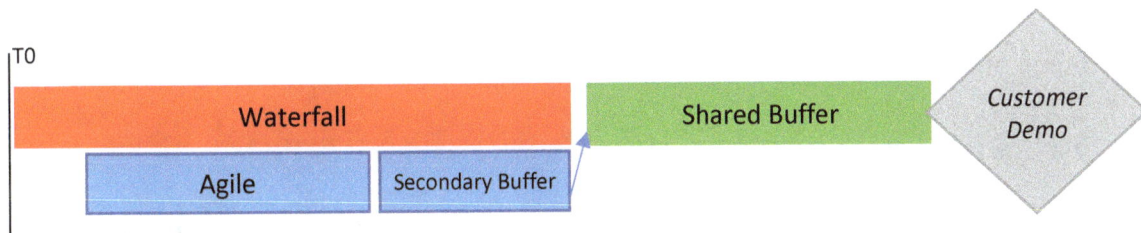

If the Agile part is delayed, the secondary buffer is therefore consumed, and the critical path changes and is positioned on the project part executed in Agile. To be on time according to the due date agreed with the customer (the actual delivery date managed), the common buffer begins to be consumed by the Agile team:

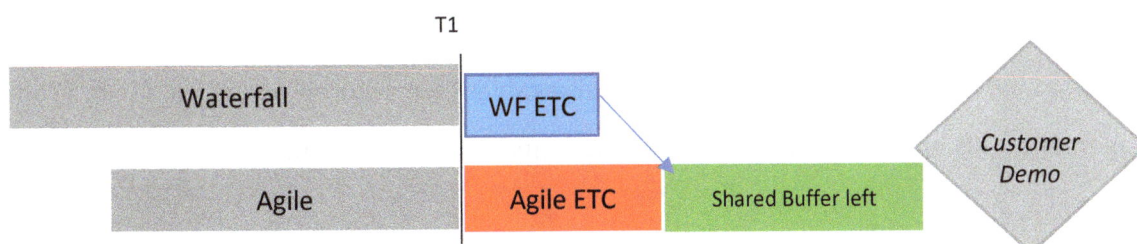

By adapting the existing practice of Critical Chain to hybrid projects accordingly, it is possible to manage teams working with different approaches on the same project.

For effective portfolio management and for shared resources perspective, it is necessary for all projects to be executed in Critical Chain Project Management (CCPM) to have a visual, unique portfolio management tool and an objective and global resource allocation: the "Fever Chart".

- ## Methodological framework

How can the Critical Chain be the appropriate tool to reconcile hybrid projects?

Note: In this analysis, hybridization means that on the two parts of the same project, one is in Waterfall, the other is in Agile, and they must be conducted in parallel.

Getting rid of constraints and maintaining the best of both approaches.

Keep only the unavoidable, imposed, non-negotiable constraints. For example, the due date of the final deliverable, the integration/synchronization/test point between sub-projects, etc. Remove false constraints, such as process review dates and resource availability, avoid fixed dates at the end of each process phase to aggregate a single commitment in each project, remove the fixed time effort...

A similarity: the difficulty in estimating

Whatever the approach, the difficulty of correctly estimating durations and complexity persists. It, therefore, results in an important imprecision, where everyone prefers to add security so as not to put himself in difficulty.

We must not have the ambition to find the right estimate. The estimates are always wrong!

The critical Chain method allows us to manage projects by accepting these uncertainties.

- ## Human dimension

Client impact: Commitments with the client (deliverables) are secured by Critical Chain Project Management. This approach helps clients to be confident in project management done by the project manager and his team. Sharing the "Fever Chart" gives it the necessary visibility on project progress.

Project team impact: With Critical Chain, we break the barriers between the two teams of the same hybrid project and align their operating modes, putting flexibility. The meetings adopt a common language ("still to be done to finish / ETC", buffer consumption) and a single indicator, the "Fever Chart". The project manager pilots the two teams, one Waterfall and the other Agile, in a homogeneous way.

- ### Conclusion

Coming from the Theory of Constraints, particularly applied in the industrial world of production and in the management of flows facilitated at the level of bottlenecks, Critical Chain Project Management applies to the Waterfall approach. It is also adapted in Agile mode, proposing a global macro-planning framework. Therefore, as part of the combination of the two approaches, **it is recommended practice in hybrid mode.**

The main benefits of Critical Chain in hybrid projects are:

- **Reconciliation** of two traditionally perceived opposing project management approaches
- **Possibility for each team to continue working in a well-known mode** (no interference) while being able **to interface** with a team that works differently.
- **Establishment of a common language** within teams.
- **Synchronization** of teamwork on shared project deliverables.
- Focus on the **Estimate To Complete (ETC)**, the "what is still to be done to finish" to keep a synthetic and real (more accurate) view of the project delivery progress.
- Use of a **single indicator**, the "Fever Chart" as an effective monitoring tool in all circumstances.

3. Glossary

- **Definition of Done (DoD):** Set of criteria to be met to be able to consider a user story or a task as completed (developed, tested, validated, accepted, transferred).

- **Definition of Ready (DoR):** Set of criteria for defining a user story or task (context, constraints, clarity of definition, estimates, etc.).

- **Key Performance Indicator (KPI):** Numerical element used to assess the performance of a process/service.

- **Objectives and Key Results (OKR):** It is a management system for defining objectives, breaking them down at all levels, and associating them with key results that must be monitored. These contribute to the achievement of the objective.

- **Buffer:** Mutualization in time measure of the margins distributed over the various tasks of the project to avoid wasting them and facilitate management (see definition of the Fever Chart). The project buffer is modeled as a task to protect a key commitment date in a project (end of a project, invoicing, deliverables, etc.)

- **Tunnel effect:** it is often associated with a single delivery at the end of the (long) project, which means that users only have visibility on the deliverable very late, hence a high risk of unpleasant surprises.

- **Fever chart** (visual project progress chart): A chart that visualizes the "health" of the project, showing the status of the project when it was last updated. It materializes the buffer index by positioning the percentage of advancement of the critical chain on the abscissa and the percentage of buffer consumption on the ordinate. At the level of a project portfolio, this graph visualizes the "health" of the project portfolio, indicating at a given moment the position of each of the projects constituting it.

- **Theory of Constraints (TOC):** Theory was developed by E. Goldratt and explained in the book "The Goal".

- **Critical chain:** the practice of project management (combining repository, behaviors, rules, and tools) to manage contingencies and complete projects "on time". The concept of a critical chain in a schedule represents the longest chain of tasks based on the functional link (critical path) and on the capacity of the resources.

- **CCPM**: "Critical Chain Project Management": project management by the Critical Chain - Some links:

  https://dantotsupm.com/2013/08/09/respecter-ses-delais-en-projet-cest-possible-par-isabelle-icord/

  https://www.proccconseil.com/_files/ugd/33a18e_a0d2654eee7e4f77b11f7c3edd8a8791.pdf

- **Stacey Matrix:** Tool allowing to know the degree of complexity of a situation according to two axes 1- the level of uncertainty of the "what" (objectives, scope, achievements of the project) and 2- the level of agreement with the situation (context of achievement projects): the "how."

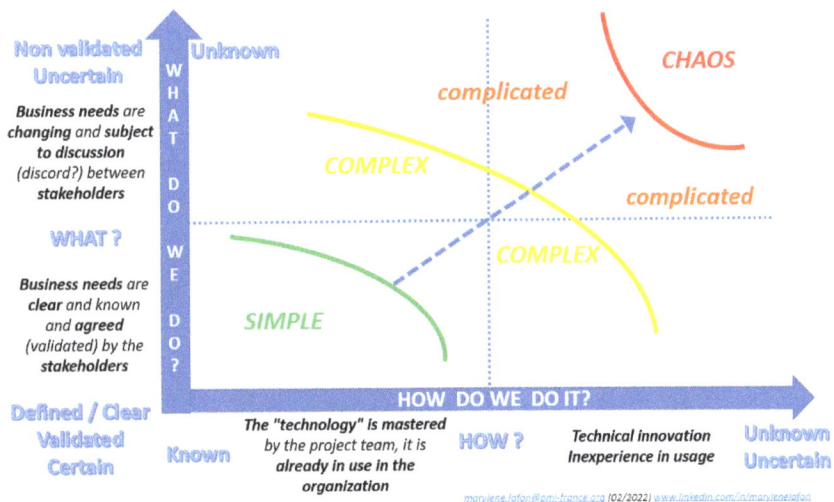

- **Project Scope:** Defines the content of the project.

- **Product Backlog:** The product backlog is a prioritized list of items or features needed to achieve goals or set expectations within an Agile team.

- **MVP (Minimum Viable Product): a** version of a product that achieves the maximum customer return (satisfaction) for the minimum effort.

- **PMO (Project Management Office):** Project control tower.

- **Tollgate:** Decision review placed in the project at key moments of its roadmap (end of a phase, major deliverable, etc.), using a checklist for which all the criteria must be completed and validated to obtain the Go.

www.ingramcontent.com/pod-product-compliance
Lightning Source LLC
Chambersburg PA
CBHW081748200326
41597CB00024B/4438